W9-CLW-254

Young Entrepreneurs

Run Your Own
Recycling Business

Emma Carlson Berne

PowerKiDS
press.

New York

Published in 2014 by The Rosen Publishing Group, Inc.
29 East 21st Street, New York, NY 10010

First Edition

Editor: Joanne Randolph
Book Design: Andrew Povolny
Book Layout: Joe Carney
Photo Research: Katie Stryker

Photo Credits: Cover Jupiterimages/Brand X Pictures/Getty Images; p. 5 Serenethos/Shutterstock.com; p. 6 Kali Nine LLC/E+/Getty Images; p. 7 Antlio/Shutterstock.com; pp. 8, 15, 22, 25 iStockphoto/Thinkstock; p. 9 JGI/Jamie Grill/Blend Images/Getty Images; p. 11 Jupiterimages/Goodshoot/Thinkstock; p. 13 Comstock Images/Thinkstock; p. 16 Nic Neish/Shutterstock.com; p. 18 Richard I'Anson/Lonely Planet Images/Getty Images; p. 19 Valueline/Thinkstock; p. 21 ImagesBazaar/The Agency Collection/Getty Images; p. 23 Jupiterimages/Brand X Pictures/Thinkstock; pp. 24, 27, 30 Fuse/Thinkstock; p. 26 Jupiterimages/Creatas/Thinkstock; p. 28 Martin Poole/Digital Vision/Thinkstock.

Library of Congress Cataloging-in-Publication Data

Berne, Emma Carlson.
  Run your own recycling business / Emma Carlson Berne. — First Edition.
     pages cm. — (Young entrepreneurs)
  Includes index.
  ISBN 978-1-4777-2923-6 (library binding) — ISBN 978-1-4777-3012-6 (pbk.) —
ISBN 978-1-4777-3083-6 (6-pack)
  1. Recycling industry. 2. New business enterprises—Management. 3. Entrepreneurship.
I. Title.
  HD9975.A2B47 2014
  363.72'82068—dc23

Manufactured in the United States of America

CPSIA Compliance Information: Batch #W14PK2: For Further Information contact Rosen Publishing, New York, New York at 1-800-237-9932

Contents

Becoming an Entrepreneur   4

Consider Recycling!   6

Make a Plan   8

The Big Budget   12

Advertising Is Key   16

Hiring Help   20

Well Supplied   24

Open for Business!   26

Are You Ready?   30

Glossary   31

Index   32

Websites   32

Becoming an Entrepreneur

Maybe you're interested in having more spending money. Maybe you're saving up for a big purchase. Have you considered opening your own business?

"That's for adults!" you might say. Actually, kids can become **entrepreneurs**, too. In this book, we will discuss the steps you can follow to run your very own business, including finding a **demand**, or need, for a good or service, making a plan, organizing and opening the business, and managing the business.

Instead of asking your parents for more money or waiting for your birthday, why don't you start earning right now? Become a young entrepreneur.

Some small businesses sell their goods or offer their services at fairs. These kinds of businesses and have lower costs since there is no need to rent permanent space to sell the goods or services.

Consider Recycling!

Before you can start your business, you need to decide what you're going to provide. Will you offer a service? Do you have a product to sell? Look around you at your community. Do you see any needs or wants that are going unfulfilled? Maybe you can provide one of these.

In the following chapters, we'll discuss how to organize and run your own recycling business.

If you think you have a good idea for a business, you might want to visit the library to find out more about that business. It will help you plan if you understand more about how your business works.

Many goods that people use are recyclable. If people separate these items from their garbage, they go to recycling plants to get processed and reused. Your business will be the first step on this path.

Bottles and cans and sometimes paper that people throw out can be collected and **redeemed** for cash at recycling centers or bottle donation centers. Recycling is good for the environment, too, since the recyclables do not go into landfills.

7

Make a Plan

Every good business starts with a plan. Grab a pen and paper and do some thinking. You will want to make lists of the supplies you will need and the types of items you want to collect for recycling.

Consider how you will obtain your recyclables. This will help you determine the supplies you'll need. Will you have a neighbor drop off cans and bottles at your house?

Write down your plan in a notebook or save it as a document on your computer. You can use your computer to research the kinds of items that can be recycled, too.

Smartphones, which have Internet access, can be used to do some research, too. You can look up prices of some of the supplies you'll need.

You'll need large bins to collect the items and signs to indicate what should go where.

Are you going to go house-to-house to gather the recyclables? In that case, you'll need to organize a way to transport the items. Do you have a wagon, a wheelbarrow, or a trailer for your bike? Will you need access to a car? Think through how the whole process, from collection to turning the goods in at a recycling center, will really work.

You'll also need to determine exactly what you are going to collect. Look online for your nearest recycling or scrap metal center. Then call and ask what they will accept in return for cash. Do they take bottles and cans? Will they accept paper also? Sometimes paper has to be brought to a different place than cans and bottles do. Do they pay for any other items?

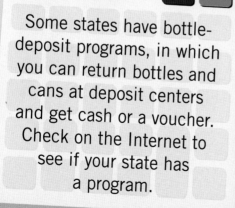

Tip Central

Some states have bottle-deposit programs, in which you can return bottles and cans at deposit centers and get cash or a voucher. Check on the Internet to see if your state has a program.

Remember to talk to your parents about your business idea and your plan to make it work. If you need their help with rides or with a loan to get you started, you will want to discuss those things as well.

The Big Budget

Now it's time to figure out your **budget**. How much money are you going to **invest**, or spend, on your business? How much do you expect to get out of your business? Entrepreneurs know they need to spend money in order to make money. You will want to spend as little as possible, though, so that you can maximize your **profits**.

When you look at the difference between your savings and your expenses, you may find that your costs are more than your savings. When you borrow money, you can estimate how much you are likely to make each month and include that data in your payment plan to repay what you owe.

Expenses	
Advertising Supplies	$15.00
Recycling Supplies (including gloves, bins, garbage bags)	$55.00
Gas Money for Transport	$10.00
Total	**$80.00**

Capital	
Savings	$65.00
Total	**$65.00**

Expenses – Capital = Total to Borrow

$80.00 – $65.00 = $15.00

Tip Central

Don't forget to **estimate** how much you'll need to collect to make a profit! Get a price for the recyclables from the center you plan to sell to.

A wagon could be a helpful tool in collecting recyclables. Try to borrow one if you do not have one. If you need to buy one, be sure to include that cost in your budget.

To create your budget, make a list of everything you will need to start and run your business. Don't forget to include things like advertising supplies and money for gas if you need car rides. Then circle everything on the list that you will need to buy or rent. Estimate how much each circled item will cost and add it all up. The total is the amount you need to put into your business.

Consider how much money you already have saved. If the total money you need is more than your savings, you will need to go into **debt**, probably to your parents. Write down how much you borrowed and when you plan to pay them back.

When you use your own money to start your business, you are investing in it. Include the amount of cash you are starting with in your budget. Is it enough to cover your start-up costs?

Advertising Is Key

Your city might already pick up recyclables at the curb, or your neighbors might take them to the recycling center themselves. Why then should people give you their cans and bottles? You're going to have to convince them through advertising.

Advertising your business serves two purposes.

You can make your own signs with craft supplies, or you can type something up on your family's computer. If you make your signs by hand, be sure to write clearly and large enough for people to be able to read them easily.

It gives your future customers practical information about your service, such as where and when you collect recyclables. It also showcases how useful your business is. Think of the benefits you can offer your customers. You could offer to pay your customers a percentage of the money you will receive from their recyclables.

Tip Central

Discuss with your parents what contact information you're allowed to put on your flyer. Is your home phone number okay? What about your email address or cell phone number?

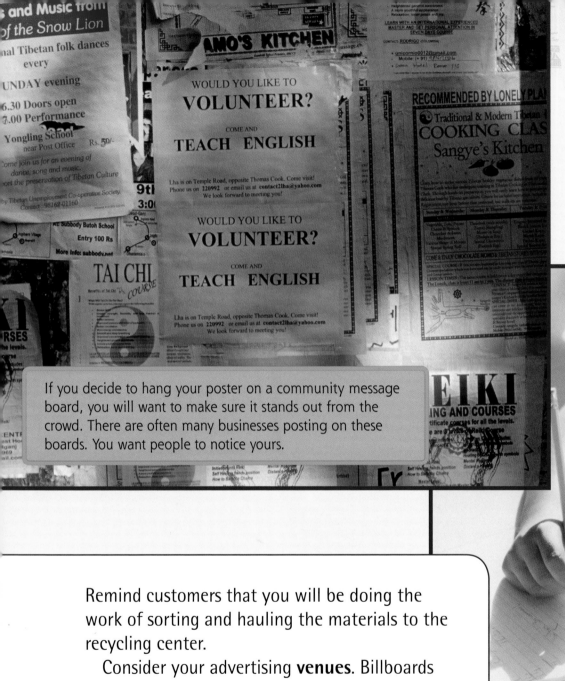

If you decide to hang your poster on a community message board, you will want to make sure it stands out from the crowd. There are often many businesses posting on these boards. You want people to notice yours.

Remind customers that you will be doing the work of sorting and hauling the materials to the recycling center.

Consider your advertising **venues**. Billboards and radio and TV commercials are probably a little outside your budget. You can probably afford to print out flyers, though.

Identify the streets from which you want to gather your recyclables. Then dress neatly and knock on each door.

With a smile, explain who you are and how your customer will benefit from your recycling business. Then hand the customer an advertising flyer.

If you show your father your advertising plan, ask him if he will send an email to his friends and neighbors telling them about your business.

Hiring Help

As you move closer to opening your business, think about organizing some **human resources**. With helpers, you might be able to collect more bottles and cans and, in the end, make more of a profit.

Consider how your **employees** can be most useful. Will you all spread out and knock on even more doors? Will you arrange the pickups and send your employees out to do the actual collecting?

You'll need to pay your employees, of course. Instead of an hourly wage, you may want to offer a percentage of the profits.

Your friends can help spread the word about your business. They can also collect the recyclables from people in their neighborhoods, help sort through them, and bring them to the recycling center.

It can be one person's job to sort the recycling. This person can make sure bottles and cans are empty, too.

Your helpers might work even harder since the more recyclables they collect, the more money they stand to gain.

You will probably also need a ride to the scrap metal or recycling center. If your parent or older sibling drives you, you'll want to offer compensation in return. Will you pay **up front** for the gas and time it takes to do the driving? You can figure out how much you owe for the gas based on how many miles away the recycling center is and finding out how many miles per gallon your parent's car gets. Chances are you will owe her at least a dollar or two each time she drives you to the center.

Working with a friend to collect recycling will make your new business more fun. Plus, it can be helpful to have another set of hands to help with anything that might be heavy.

Tip Central

If you hire help, write down the pay agreement and sign it. Then have your helper sign it also. That way, you won't have any misunderstandings about who is getting paid what when.

Well Supplied

You will need several plastic tubs to hold the recycling you collect.

It's time to go shopping! Make a list of all the supplies you'll need and figure out which you'll need to buy and which you already have or can borrow.

You'll probably need large garbage bags to stash the bottles and cans, twist ties to secure the tops, a pair of protective gloves, supplies for your advertising flyers, and most importantly, some method of transporting your recyclables.

Consider using a wagon, a wheelbarrow, or a trailer for your bicycle. You could also take more money out of your budget and pay a parent or older sibling to follow you in a car as you make the pickups.

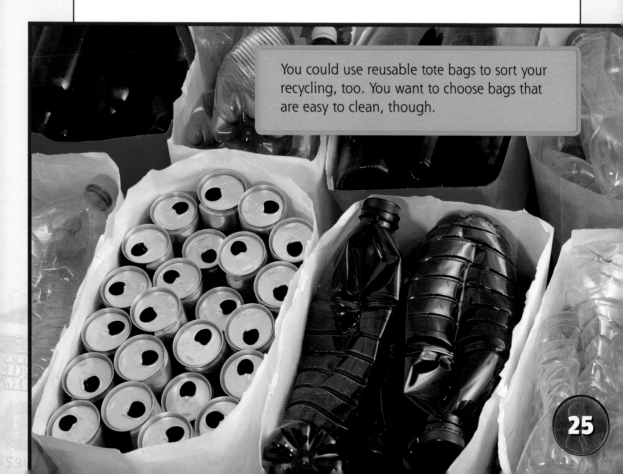

You could use reusable tote bags to sort your recycling, too. You want to choose bags that are easy to clean, though.

Open for Business!

You've hired helpers, distributed your flyers, and collected your supplies. It's time to open for business! You can schedule pickups for customers or designate a drop-off area for those who prefer to bring their recyclables to you.

Grab your recycling bin and get started. Decide if you will go to the recycling center every week to redeem what you collect for cash or if you will go every other week.

Think creatively about sources for recycling. You can organize a cleanup of your local park with your friends. You will be doing a community service, plus you can keep the recyclable materials for your business!

As you begin collecting your recyclables, whether from drop-offs at your home or by going door-to-door, carry a notebook with you in which you keep careful track of all the items you collect, whom you collect them from, and how much you are taking in.

Your business does not have to stop at paper and plastic. You can help people recycle their kitchen waste, too. Composting is easy and Earth friendly. You can sell the rich soil you create to local gardeners.

Write down any money that goes out to your helpers or to your customers and all the money that comes in.

Most importantly, keep careful track of your budget. The goal of your business is to make a profit. If you find yourself spending more money than you are taking in, you will need to increase the amount you're collecting or increase your hours. Take a few minutes every week and go over your notebook so you can make changes if necessary. Ask customers to tell their friends about your business. Every good business owner is looking for ways to expand his business and increase his profits.

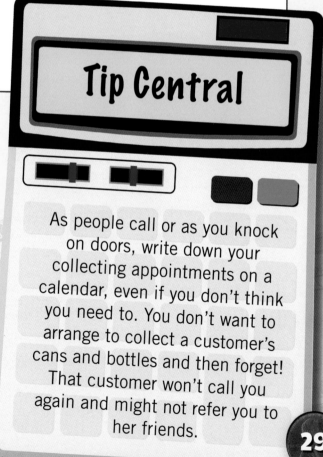

Tip Central

As people call or as you knock on doors, write down your collecting appointments on a calendar, even if you don't think you need to. You don't want to arrange to collect a customer's cans and bottles and then forget! That customer won't call you again and might not refer you to her friends.

Are You Ready?

On a separate sheet of paper, check off these items to make sure you have everything ready for your recycling business.

- ☐ Search online for your state's bottle-and-can deposit program, if there is one.
- ☐ Look online to locate the nearest bottle-and-can deposit center or recycling or scrap metal center.
- ☐ Call the center and ask what recyclables they accept and how much they pay.
- ☐ Create a budget and figure out how much money you need to borrow, if any.
- ☐ Arrange to borrow money from parents if needed and set up a payment schedule.
- ☐ Create a business plan. Decide if you will do door-to-door collecting, home drop-off, or scheduled pickups.
- ☐ Shop for supplies, including advertising materials.
- ☐ Draw up advertising flyers.
- ☐ Distribute flyers, and talk face-to-face with potential customers.
- ☐ Hire helpers and arrange payment and work schedules.
- ☐ Organize transportation for recyclable pickup and transport to recycling center.
- ☐ Carefully record money spent and money earned.
- ☐ Collect your recyclables and enjoy your profits!

Glossary

budget (BUH-jit) A plan to spend a certain amount of money in a period of time.

debt (DET) Something owed.

demand (dih-MAND) A need or want people have for a good or a service.

employees (im-ploy-EEZ) People who are paid to work for a person or a business.

entrepreneurs (on-truh-pruh-NURZ) Businesspeople who have started their own business.

estimate (ES-teh-mayt) To make a guess based on knowledge or facts.

human resources (HYOO-mun REE-sors-ez) The efforts of people who make goods and provide services.

invest (in-VEST) To put money into something, such as a company, in the hope of getting more money later on.

profits (PRAH-fits) The money a company makes after all its bills are paid.

redeemed (rih-DEEMD) Exchanged.

up front (UP FRUNT) In advance.

venues (VEN-yooz) Areas or places where things happen.

Index

A
adults, 4

B
bottles, 7–8, 10, 16, 20, 25

C
cans, 7–8, 10, 16, 20, 25
community, 6

D
debt, 14
demand, 4

E
employees, 20

G
gas, 14, 22
good(s), 4, 9

H
human resources, 20

M
money, 4, 12, 14, 17, 22, 25, 29–30

P
paper, 7–8, 10
plan, 4, 8, 14, 30
product, 6
profit(s), 12, 20, 29–30
purchase, 4

R
recyclables, 7–9, 16–17, 19–20, 22, 25–27, 30
recycling center(s), 7, 9, 16, 18, 22, 30

Websites

Due to the changing nature of Internet links, PowerKids Press has developed an online list of websites related to the subject of this book. This site is updated regularly. Please use this link to access the list:
www.powerkidslinks.com/ye/recycl/